Sleight of Hand

GUITAR MAGIC

Solo Guitar Arrangements
for the
Partial Capo

HARVEY REID

WOODPECKER
MULTIMEDIA
York, Maine USA

Music copy: Jeff Hickey   **Design & Graphics:** Aphro-Graphics

© 1983, 2003, 2013 by Harvey Reid. All rights reserved.

ISBN: 978-1-63029-001-6

WOODPECKER
MULTIMEDIA

PO Box 815 York Maine 03909 USA

www.woodpecker.com

TABLE OF CONTENTS

WARNING!!

All the arrangements in this book require the use of a partial capo.
The notes as written are unplayable otherwise. Be sure that you have a
partial capo properly placed in the configuration indicated in the TAB
for each song. All the arrangements in this book except *Für Elise,
Greensleeves* and *Scarborough Fair* are played in standard tuning.

ABOUT THE ARRANGEMENTS

The guitar arrangements in this book all make use of the partial capo as a way to obtain fresh and new guitar sounds. By shortening only selected strings rather than just clamping across the whole fingerboard as conventional capos do, the pitch of the open strings can be changed without changing the tuning of the guitar. The effect of using such a device can be rather startling, since it allows you to play chords and sequences of notes that would not otherwise be possible. Most of the arrangements included here are intended for a normally tuned 6-string guitar, and most of them are for a fingerpicking style, although two of the tunes were written specifically to be flatpicked, two are for 12-string guitar only, and three are for a guitar tuned to an open tuning used in conjunction with a partial capo. Many of the tunes are quite common, so as to be familiar, and to offer easy comparison with "conventional" ways of playing them. The arrangements have also been written to take maximum advantage of the new opportunities offered by the partial capo, and are almost certainly unplayable without the device.

For those who play fiddle tunes: there is, of course, no "correct" way to play any of them, and we all tend to play them even a little differently each time. If you don't know the tune, play it as written here and gradually adapt it so suit your tastes. If you already play the tune, you can easily borrow ideas here and adapt the arrangements as you see fit. I have purposely left out many of the fills, trills and ornaments that I often use, in order to keep the melodies straightforward, and you can add to them as you like, since that is what you are supposed to do with fiddle tunes.

Some of these tunes are easier than others, but they are all designed so they can be played smoothly and naturally, and not sound labored. This is the first published collection of serious guitar music for the "three-handed" guitarist, and although it is only the tip of a very big iceberg. The celtic, bluegrass, classical and folk tunes here illustrate quite well the advantages of a partial capo. I hope we will never outgrow the need for new sounds and new ways to play old songs. I hope these arrangements put a grin on your face, and help you enjoy your guitar even more.

Pick a tune... any tune...
the hand is quicker than the ear.

HARVEY REID (*April 1983*)

ABOUT THE PARTIAL CAPO

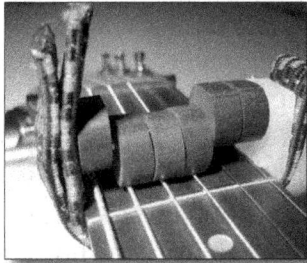

Third Hand Capo (*universal*)

Shubb c7b (*Esus/A*)

Kyser "Short Cut" (*Esus/A*)

Liberty "Flip"
(*3 or 4 inner strings*)

SpiderCapo
(*universal*)

Capos have existed for centuries as a way to raise the pitch of the guitar by clamping across all the strings. The first partial capo was the *Third Hand Capo*, which appeared in 1976. There are now 15 other partial capos that allow you to clamp only some of your strings. They all have their own musical value, and allow clamping of 1, 2, 3, 4 or 5 strings. The *Third Hand* and the *SpiderCapo* are universal: both allow you to rotate 6 "fingers" up or down to obtain 63 different options at each fret. These two are ideal for use with this book. Learn more at **www. PartialCapo.com**.

Partial capos are useful for helping beginners with simplified chord fingerings, but more advanced guitarists use them for basically the same reasons as a different tuning: to get new open strings and new resonances. Partial capos open up a large expanse of new musical possibilities, allowing things that can't be done any other way. It's easiest to think of the capo as a way of imitating the sound of non-standard tunings, though the two are by no means identical. Tunings and partial capos both have great value, and offer different sets of options. (It is possible and useful to use a partial capo and an altered tuning together, as is done in 3 of the songs in this book.) **The partial capo has a significant advantage over retuning– much of the effect of a tuning can be achieved in standard tuning, and thus without the need to relearn the fingerboard.** Since the strings have not been retuned, scales and chord geometry are unchanged.

Many of the songs in this book involve playing with familiar left-hand positions, but with open strings offering new melody options or bass support. Usually in the keys of E and A, they all take musical advantage of the new landscape of open-string options that the partial capo offers. The *Minuet in Dm*, *Fur Elise*, and *Scherzo* are all exact, note-for-note transcriptions of classical guitar pieces that would be unplayable or much more difficult otherwise.

The capo configurations used in this book:

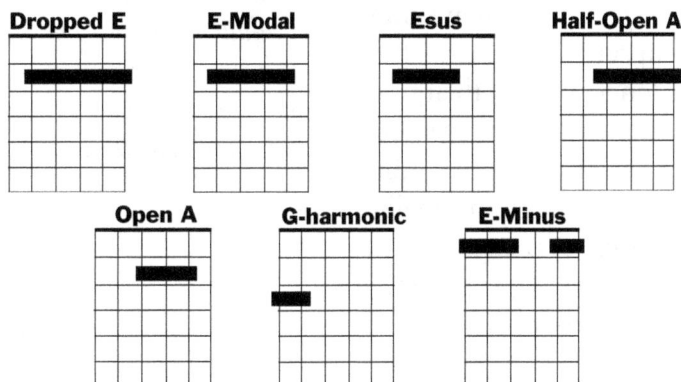

Dropped E

E-Modal

Esus

Half-Open A

Open A

G-harmonic

E-Minus

tuned: Eb-Bb-Eb-G-Bb-Eb

1

ABOUT THE NOTATION

The arrangements in this book have been written in both standard musical notation and guitar *tablature*. Tablature (TAB) is an easier system to work with for those who are not used to working with printed music, since it shows the positions of the notes on the guitar string. It does not effectively portray the "shape" of the melody, however, or the time values of the notes. That information should be obtained from the standard notation, as well as the left-hand fingering instructions that are placed next to the notes, whenever there may be confusion about the fingerings.

The partial capo is depicted on each line of TAB to remind you that it is on the guitar, and the TAB numbers indicate how many frets above the capo the notes are to be played. **An open string is played open and notated as a "0" whether or not it is a real open string or clamped by the capo.** Barre chords are written as Roman numerals above the TAB whenever their occurrence is not clear from the TAB, in the manner of classical guitar notation convention.

An extra word of caution is needed here concerning the standard notation. Whenever a different tuning of the guitar is used, it upsets the sight-reading process, since the notes no longer occupy their usual positions on the neck. Many of the arrangements here are played with the guitar in standard tuning, and although the notes could be read "normally", the capo changes the fingerings of many passages, and the TAB must be consulted even by experienced sight-readers. For those of you used to working with

a capo, it would seem more natural when playing in *Dropped-E* configuration to write a D chord played above the capo as a D chord and the open bass string as a low D, since that is what it "feels" like is going on when you are playing. In this particular instance, it might make sense to write the notes as they "feel" rather than as they sound, but since there are so many other capo configurations with unusual properties, **the only sensible thing to do is to write the notes as they actually sound.**

A few of these arrangements are in different tunings, and some may "seem" to be in keys other than where they are written. (E feels like D, for example.) This makes it easy for anyone familiar with standard notation to appreciate the unusual musical quality of these arrangements, and allows a sensible and consistent notation system. Those who are experienced at sight-reading will have to consult the TAB to play the arrangements. There should be no confusion as to how the pieces in this book should sound or be played.

NOTE: *I wrote these arrangements in 1983, before computer music software, and made my own decisions about notating for partial capos. Recently other conventions of notating partial capos have introduced more confusion into an already confusing subject.*

I have chosen to use a theta (Ø) symbol in the TAB to show a note at the same fret as the capo, and a negative number to show notes that are rarely below the capo (p.30). This is to preserve the intuitive notion of counting TAB from the capo and not the nut. Because the music notation software now available does not yet allow for the idea of partial capos, other people are publishing arrangements that count all TAB from the nut. This has the distinct disadvantage that "open" strings fretted by the capo are not shown as 0 in the TAB.

Pavanne

This is an old melody from the Renaissance that I've given first a bass line and then a simple harmony. The *Dropped-E* configuration used here allows you to play things like this in a minor key with the low root bass note, something that causes problems if you tune it down to D as is often done in such situations. The F barre chord (actually G as written here) figures prominently in the arrangement, and would not be possible if the bass string were lowered. This arrangement is not at all hard, and is a good project for someone who is just getting started playing classical-style guitar. It retains a very ancient, lute-like mood in this version.

Minuet in Dm

This one sounds in Em, but when you transcribe Bach pieces for guitar you always have to make some concessions. Actually this is the only concession made, and this arrangement is otherwise note-for-note transcribed from the keyboard version. It would not be possible to arrange this otherwise without leaving out some important notes, either in standard tuning or in the common altered tunings. It is not easy, but Bach never is on guitar, though it is quite playable and beautiful, and a good example of how useful a partial capo is for playing "legitimate" guitar.

PAVANNE

Thoinet Arbeau

MINUET IN Dm

J. S. Bach

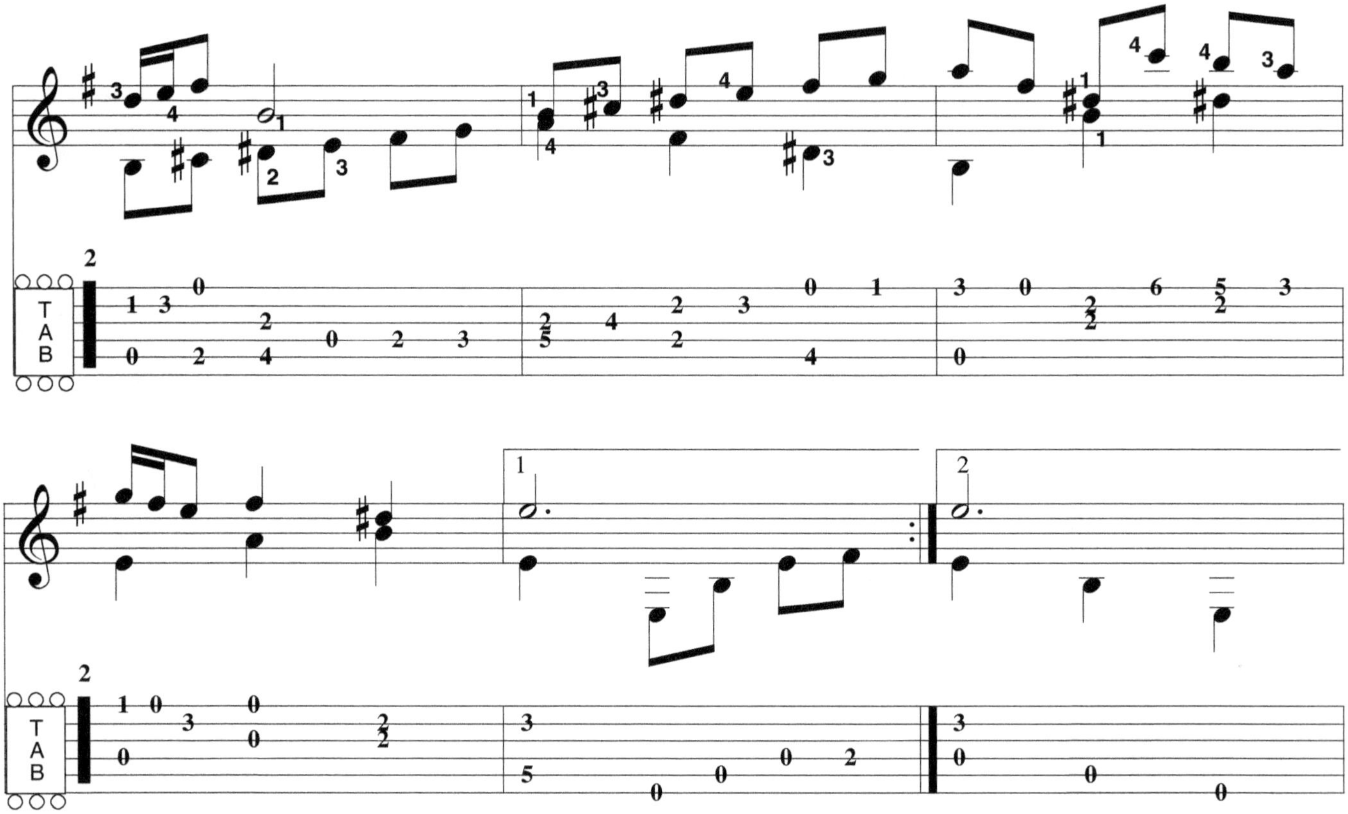
TAB
TAB

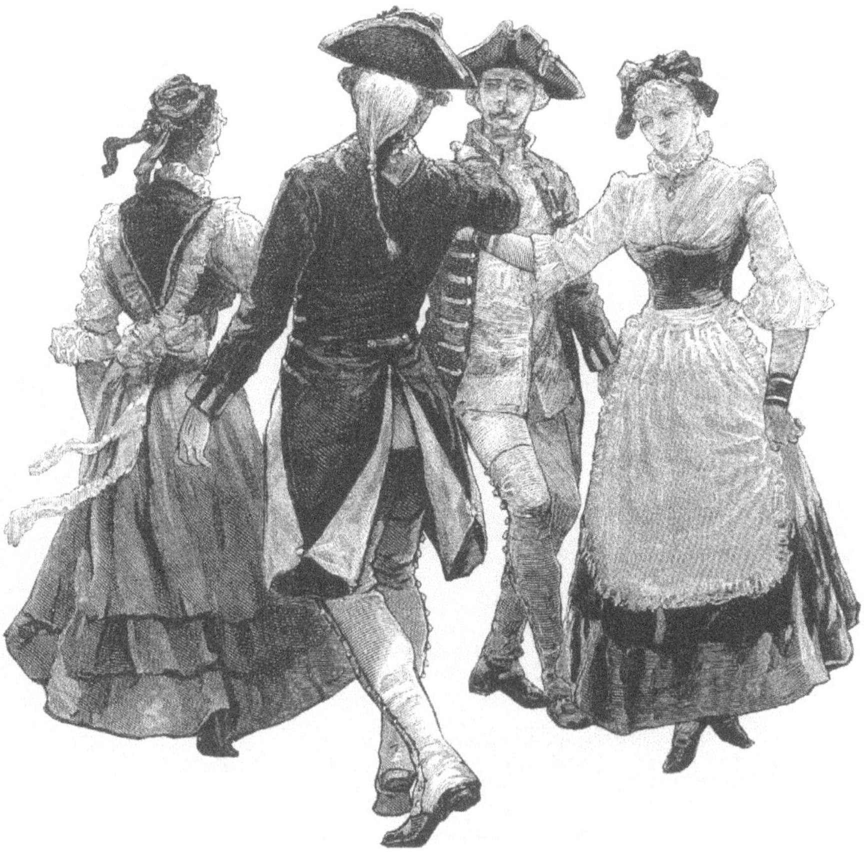

FAREWELL TO TARWAITHE

Trad.

D.C. al Fine

Farewell To Tarwaithe

Farewell To Tarwaithe (pronounced tar-wa-thie) is a very simple and hauntingly beautiful whaling song that makes a lovely instrumental, and may be familiar as the "*My horses ain't hungry, they won't eat your hay...*" family of folk songs. The open-chord sound of this configuration creates a warmth and a sustaining resonance that are very appropriate for the melody. Many of the important melody notes in the tune are consonant with the open strings, and sympathetic vibrations cause them to sound richer and sweeter than normal tuning. Here it is played in 2 octaves, and watch the timing of the melody notes as played against the drone bass, since the syncopation is what gives the tune its motion. The third time through the tune, a simple harmony is added, but feel free to experiment with other bass lines, and especially harmonics. It is possible to play this whole melody in harmonics against the drone bass, which is lovely. I recorded this on my first LP in 1982 *Nothin' But Guitar*.

E-Modal Boogie

This is basically an exercise in walking bass lines, that illustrates how easy it is to play a boogie-woogie bass line in this configuration. You never have to leave the nut position, there are no barre chords, and there is no other way to do this in standard tuning. The capo also frees up some extra fingers in your left hand, so you can keep chords and a melody going without dropping the bass line. There are, of course, hundreds of ways to "walk" a bass line like this, and an uncountable number of melody "licks" you can play against the bass line. This should get you started, and you will find that there is no simpler way to play a boogie-woogie bass line on guitar.

E-MODAL BOOGIE

H. Reid

The Flowers Of Edinburgh

This is a lovely, lilting fiddle tune from the British Isles that sounds best to my ears on guitar when played in a hornpipe rhythm, as it may have originally been done. Each pair of eighth notes should be felt as a dotted eighth note and a sixteenth note, even though hornpipes are typically written without the dotted notes. Many fiddle players play this as a fast reel in G (its original key) and you have to capo 3 frets below the partial capo and really hurry to play this along with them. This arrangement sounds better slower, and you might want to double-time the bass line for more rhythm drive. There are always plenty of open-string bass notes in the positions you'll be in, and it should be easy to fill them in if you like the sound. Barre at fret 7 in measures 5 and 6 and at fret 2 in measures 3, 4, 7, 8, 10 and 12. The "chromatic" style runs in measures 11 and 15 illustrate one of the nicest features of the *Esus* configuration, since the successive notes are all played on different strings, giving a harp-like effect.

THE FLOWERS OF EDINBURGH

Trad. Arr/ Reid.

THE RED-HAIRED BOY

Trad. Arr/ Reid.

The Red-Haired Boy

Also known as "*The Little Beggarman*," this is a very well-known fiddle tune that is usually played as a fast reel in A. It was probably also originally a hornpipe, and has a more natural and Irish feel on guitar when played with a dotted-note rhythm. Hammer-ons, pull-offs, and trills are very much a part of Irish music, and can be added almost anywhere. If you are a flatpicker, you can also play this arrangement and ignore the bass notes, or hit them when you have time. Most celtic guitarists tune their guitars to suspended tunings (D-A-D-G-A-D most often) to obtain the haunting resonances that are typical of this music, and here the Esus configuration mimics that sound almost perfectly, though it does sound in E. If you tune the guitar down a whole step, it is almost impossible to tell this is not DADGAD tuning, since the strings also have a similar slack tone.

JUNE APPLE

Trad.

June Apple

"*June Apple*," like the two previous tunes, is very common among American (especially Appalachian) fiddlers, who play it very fast in the key of A. Once again, it sounds much more celtic and natural if you play it with a bouncy, hornpipe dotted rhythm. The droning high E string, when played against the D chord creates the same effect as the 5th string of a banjo. The second half (B part) of the tune sounds great when played in a higher octave up the neck, though it is not written here. If you capo the whole guitar up 3 (or even 5 if you have a cutaway guitar) before putting on the partial capo, you get a very sweet tone, that I prefer to the key of E version with the open E strings. This can sound very reminiscent of frailing banjo, especially if you slur and pull-off the notes like they do in that style. In fact, this arrangement sounds fabulous on a 6-string banjo, which is tuned like a guitar.

JESU, JOY OF MAN'S DESIRING

JS Bach

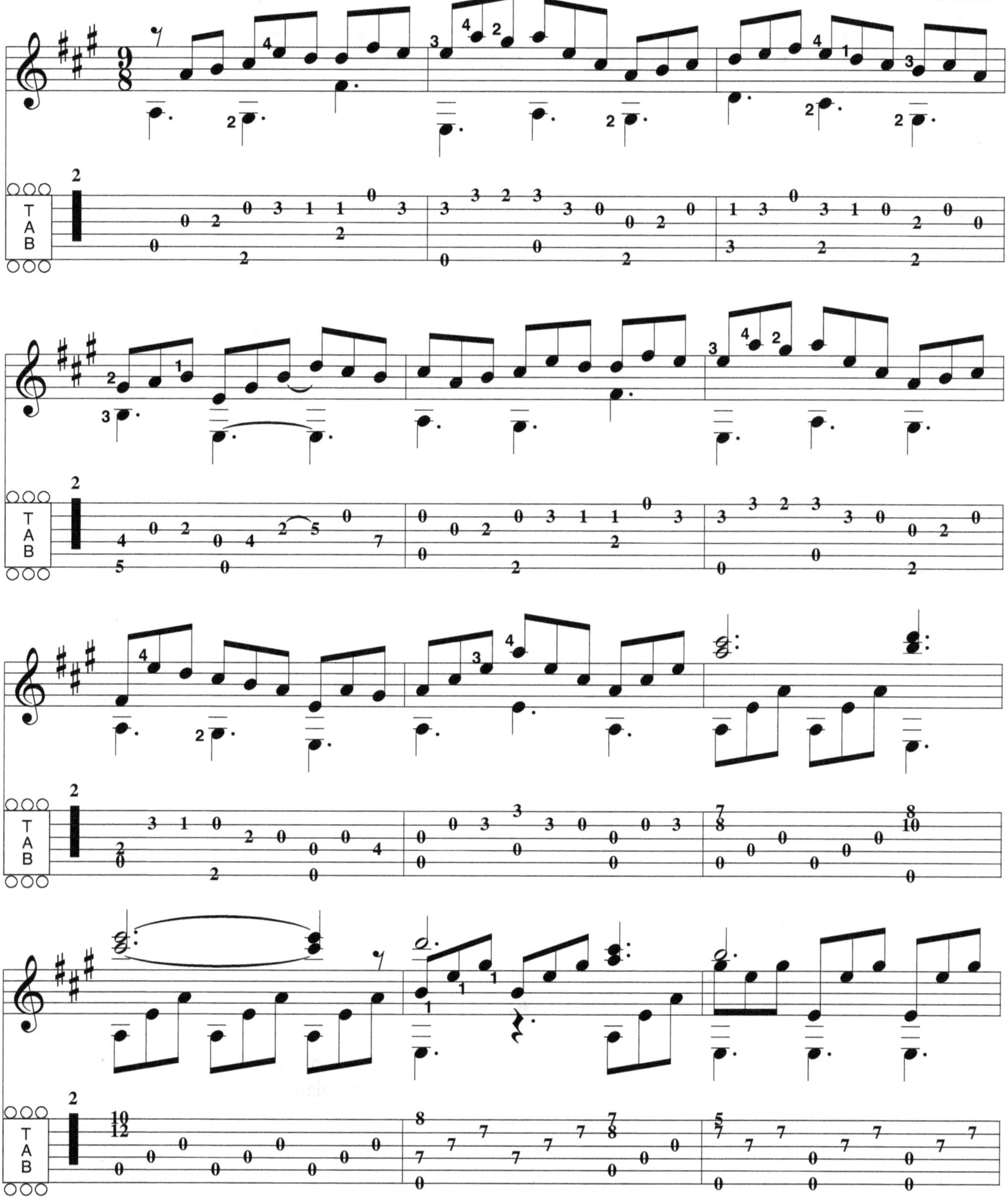

Jesu, Joy Of Man's Desiring

There are many transcriptions of this piece, for all kinds of instruments. The section here is the most commonly heard portion of what was a J.S. Bach choral work, with Latin words. Although this arrangement is by no means complete or rigorous, it is easy to play and sounds lovely. It is intended to be similar in sound to Leo Kottke's recording of the tune in *Open G* tuning, although this sounds a whole step higher in A. It features slightly different bass lines and arpeggios, as you might expect for something in a different tuning. There are no fast runs or hard left-hand stretches, and everybody likes this tune.

Simple Gifts

"*Simple Gifts*" is familiar to many as a selection from Aaron Copland's "*Appalachian Spring*." The tune comes from a European dance, probably a quadrille, possibly Scandinavian. It has words that were added in Maine in 1848, by the New England religious sect the Shakers. Some people even call it "*Tis A Gift to Be Simple*." It is often played on open-tuned instruments such as the banjo or dulcimer, and is given here in a droning version, played in two octaves on the guitar. Because of the open-string bass support, the tune does not lose strength when you play in the higher positions. I recorded this in 1982 on *Nothin' But Guitar* and again in 1994 on *Chestnuts*.

SIMPLE GIFTS

Trad. Arr/ Reid.

Higher Octave

THE IRISH WASHERWOMAN

Trad. Arr/ Reid.

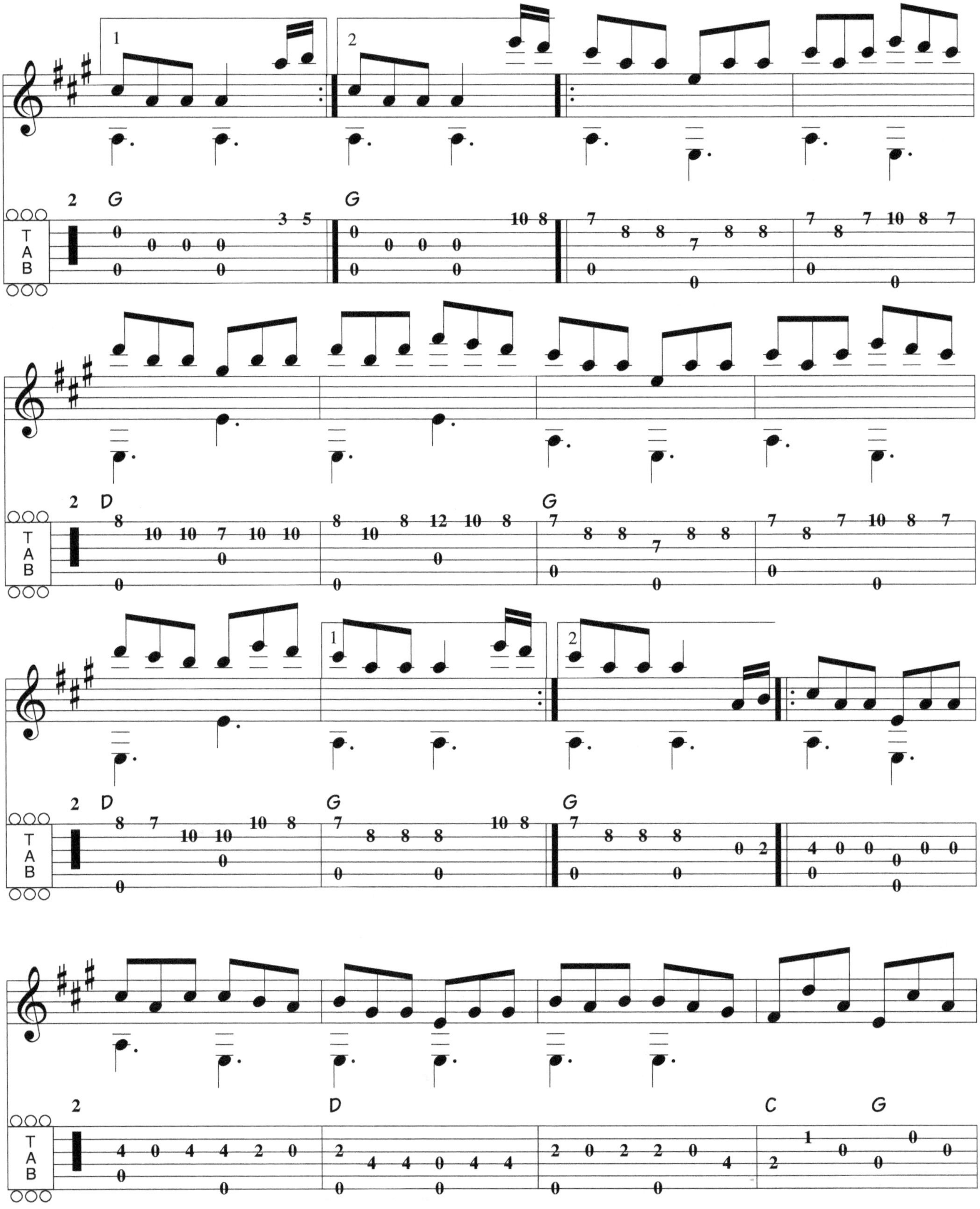
G
G
TAB
D
G
TAB
D
G
G
TAB
D
C
G
TAB

The Irish Washerwoman

This is the melody familiar to us as the "Irish Jig", and it has dozens of humorous verses. Because so many of the bass notes and melody notes are open strings, you can play this pretty fast. The extra left-hand freedom you have should enable you to play it smoothly, which is important for this kind of tune, which should not sound choppy or labored. The high-octave part is quite a bit harder than the low octave, and you will hold a barre across the top three strings throughout the entire first half of the higher-octave section. The second half is given here is the low octave for variety, although a performance version of this might make use of a different mix of high and low octave sections.

Devil's Dream

"*Devil's Dream*" is an extremely common tune that fiddlers play in the key of A. It is one of the few that guitar flatpickers will play in open A position, since the opening riff is almost impossible to play effectively in G with a capo. This arrangement is similar to Dan Crary's, and is designed for flatpick style. It's a lot easier to play this way than in standard tuning A position, since the capo does a lot of the barring for you. Some of the runs here are typical of the way the tune is heard on the guitar, and some of them are designed to take advantage of the new open strings offered by the partial capo. This arrangement makes the cross-picking section easier, and also allows you to play the A-part melody in the bass, something that isn't done by even the best "two-handed" pickers.

Sally Goodin'

"*Sally Goodin*" is usually played by fiddlers in A, so you will be able to jump right into the "parking lot picker" sessions with this one. You'll hear this tune many different ways, of course, although you will need a partial capo to make it sound like this. The tune only has 2 chords, so you can take maximum advantage of the open-chord resonance, and make your guitar ring like a banjo. The slides in measures 6 and 7 will seem tricky at first, but make for good bluegrass music. If you are good, you can play the first half of this tune up an octave and the second half down an octave, and still keep the drone-chord resonance throughout. You can really unwind on this one, and there are all kinds of cross-picking things you can do on the middle strings, similar to Scruggs banjo style rolls, chokes and pull-offs.

DEVIL'S DREAM

Trad. Arr/ Reid.

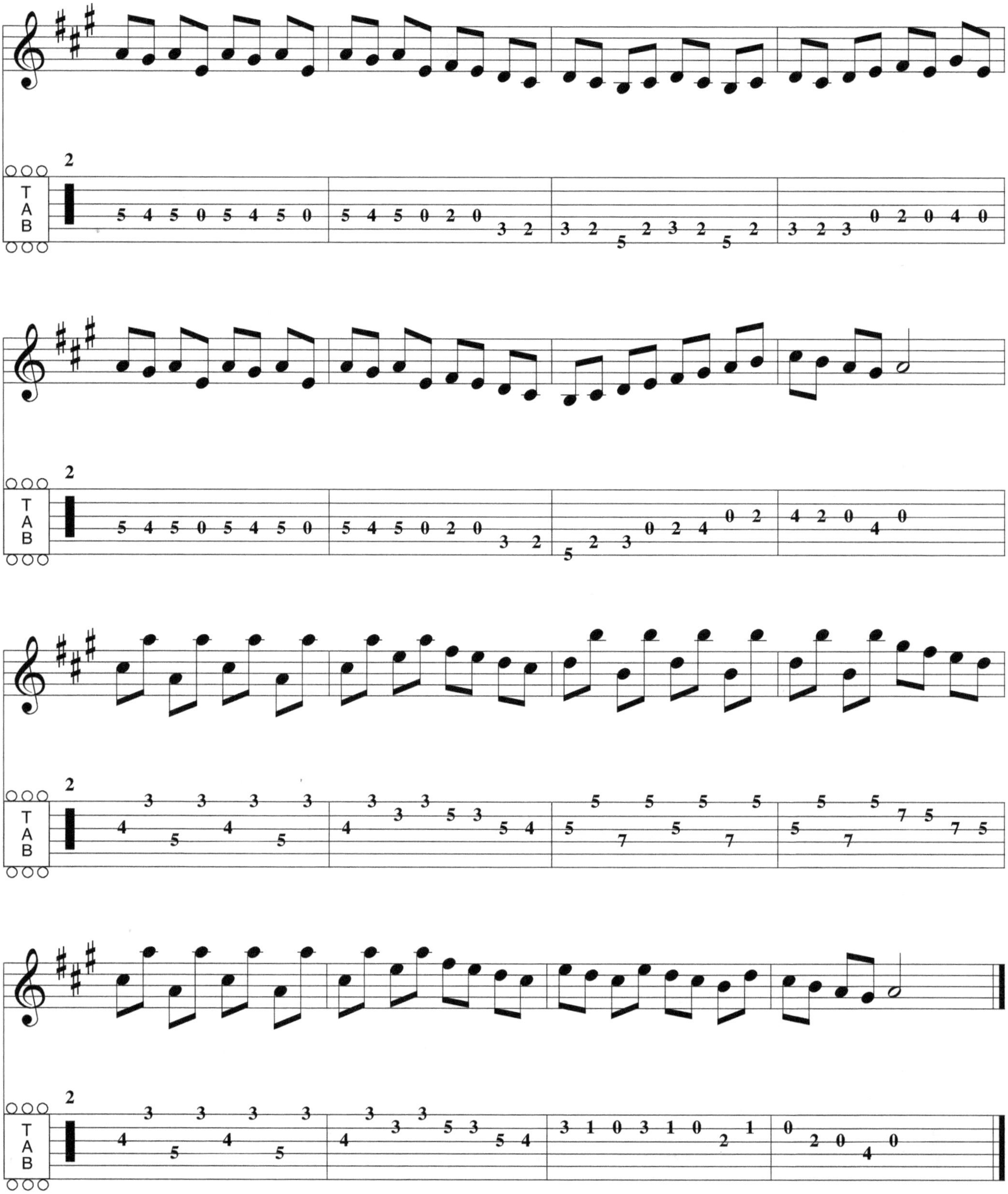

SALLY GOODIN'

Trad. Arr/ Reid.

SCHERZO

Damas- Tarrega

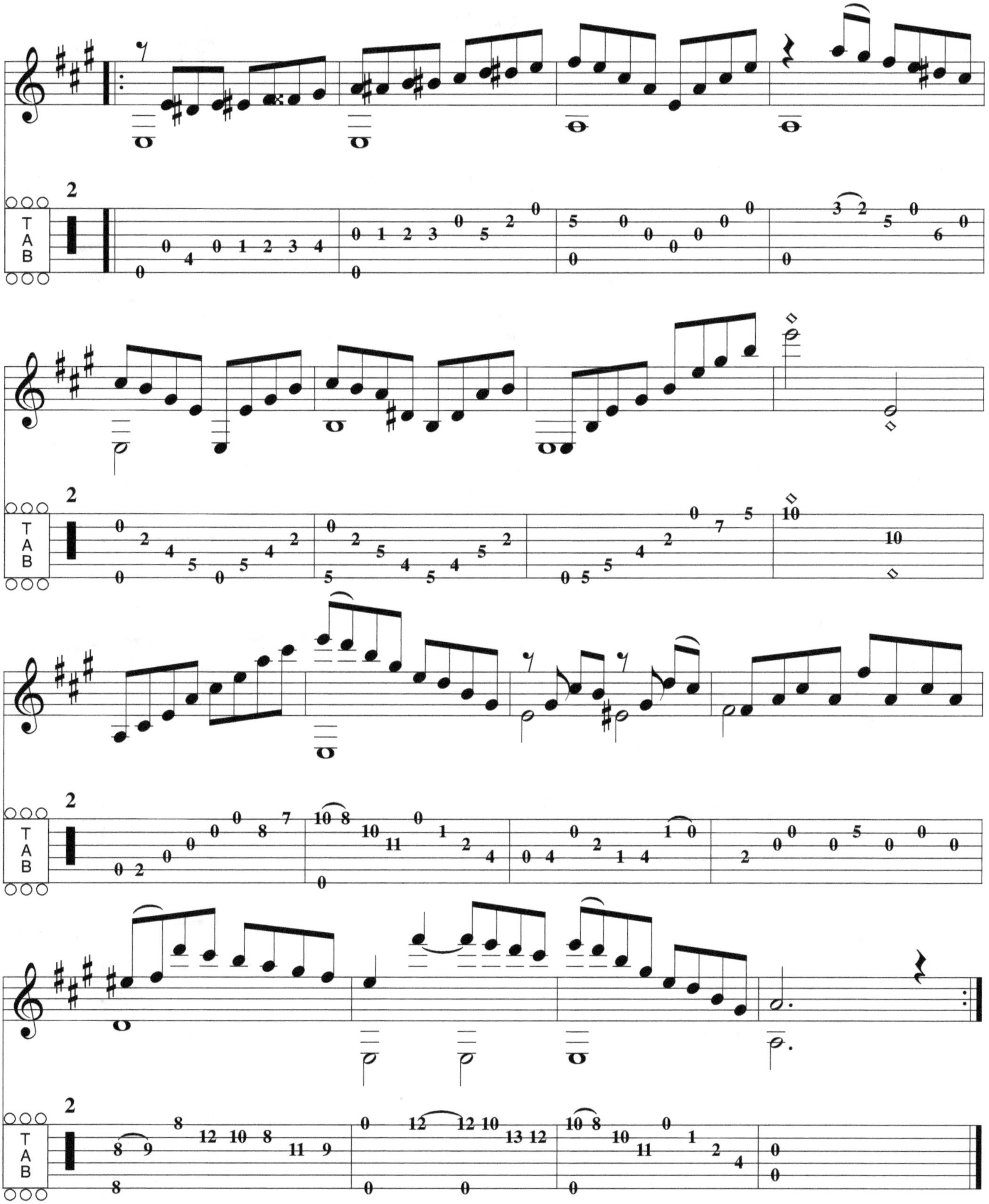

TAB

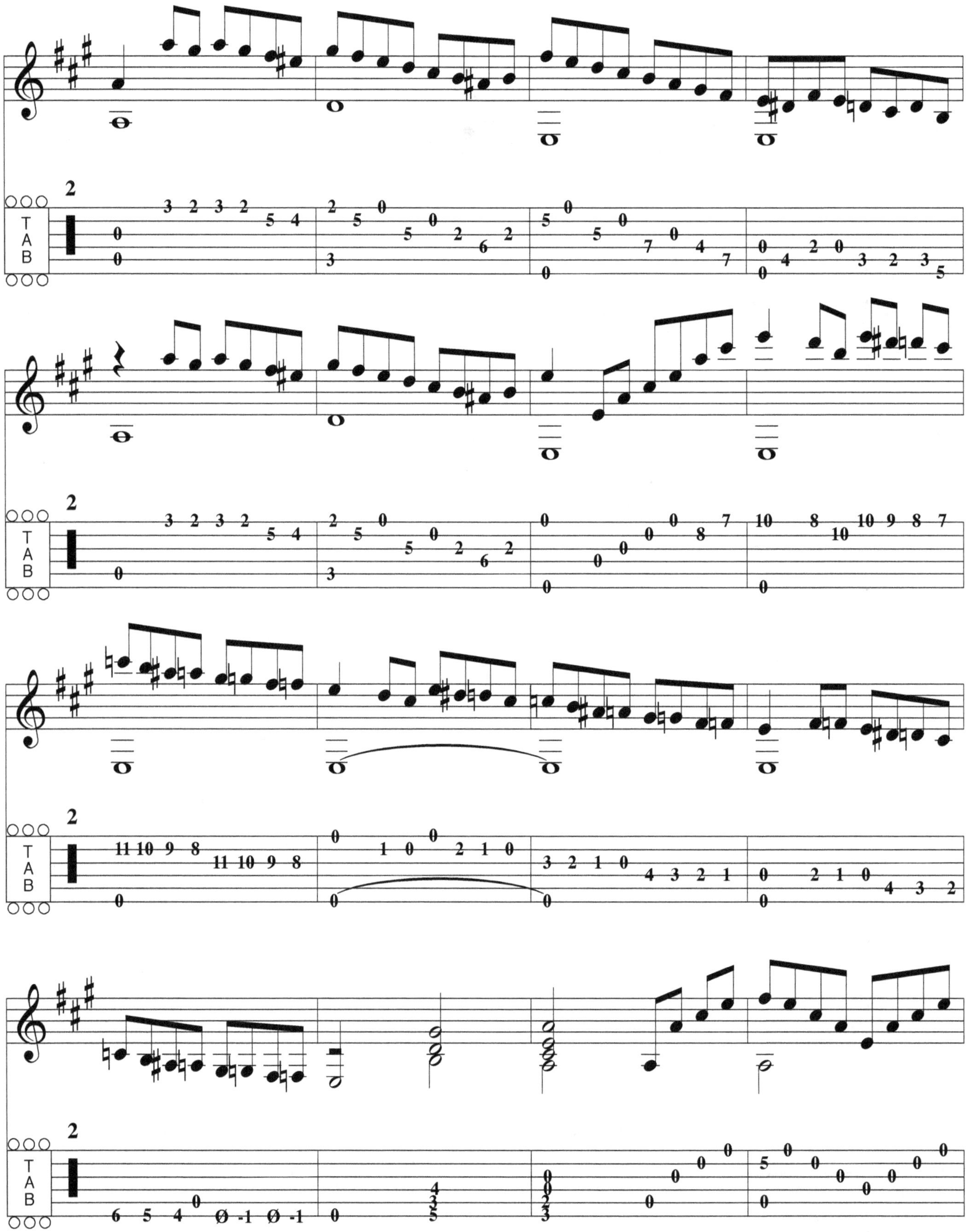

Scherzo

This piece was written for a standard-tuned guitar long before a partial capo ever existed, but it seems much easier to play if you use one. A quick glance at the arrangement shows you how many of the notes are open strings. This isn't easy, but it sounds very natural and flowing. You'll need a good right-hand arpeggio, and in measure 13 of the third page, two of the notes land behind the capo. If you are using a *Third Hand Capo*, you can reach these notes better if you remove the rubber discs that are not in use. With a 3-string *Esus* capo, it is much easier to reach over it. This is a great show-off trick if people are watching closely.

Shenandoah

This arrangement of this classic folk melody consists entirely of harmonics, so all the notes sound an octave higher than they are written. **Do not play fretted notes at the fret numbers indicated by the TAB.** This unusual capo configuration allows you to play an entire G scale in harmonics, and also gives you an open-string bass root note for the I, IV and V chords, for a full sound. This beautiful arrangement cannot be played any other way, and sounds best on a steel-string guitar. The idea is to play the bass notes as open strings, while playing the melody entirely as harmonics.

SHENANDOAH

Trad. Arr/ Reid.

32

Scarborough Fair

The "E-Minus" configuration, as I call this, adds a totally new and unique flavor to the guitar for playing in minor keys. When you actually tune to a minor chord, there are many great inconveniences in fingering, but here, since the guitar is tuned major, you get major chords whenever you barre across the fingerboard. The open minor chord has a very ancient, lute-like voicing to it, and the warmth and resonance you get here make it one of the most interesting and beautiful uses of a partial capo. The melody is played in 2 octaves, and though the higher octave is considerably harder, it does not lose any of its fullness. Measure 2 of the 3rd page has a long stretch, but it is not as hard as it looks.

Greensleeves

"*Greensleeves*" is one of the oldest, most familiar and most beautiful songs in all of Western music, and has been arranged effectively for almost every instrument. This new arrangement in the E-Minus configuration has some ancient-sounding drone resonances and a haunting mood, with unusual and exquisite (but satisfying) chord voicings. It is not at all difficult, and is richer-sounding than any "two-handed" version I have ever heard.

SCARBOROUGH FAIR

Trad. Arr/ Reid.

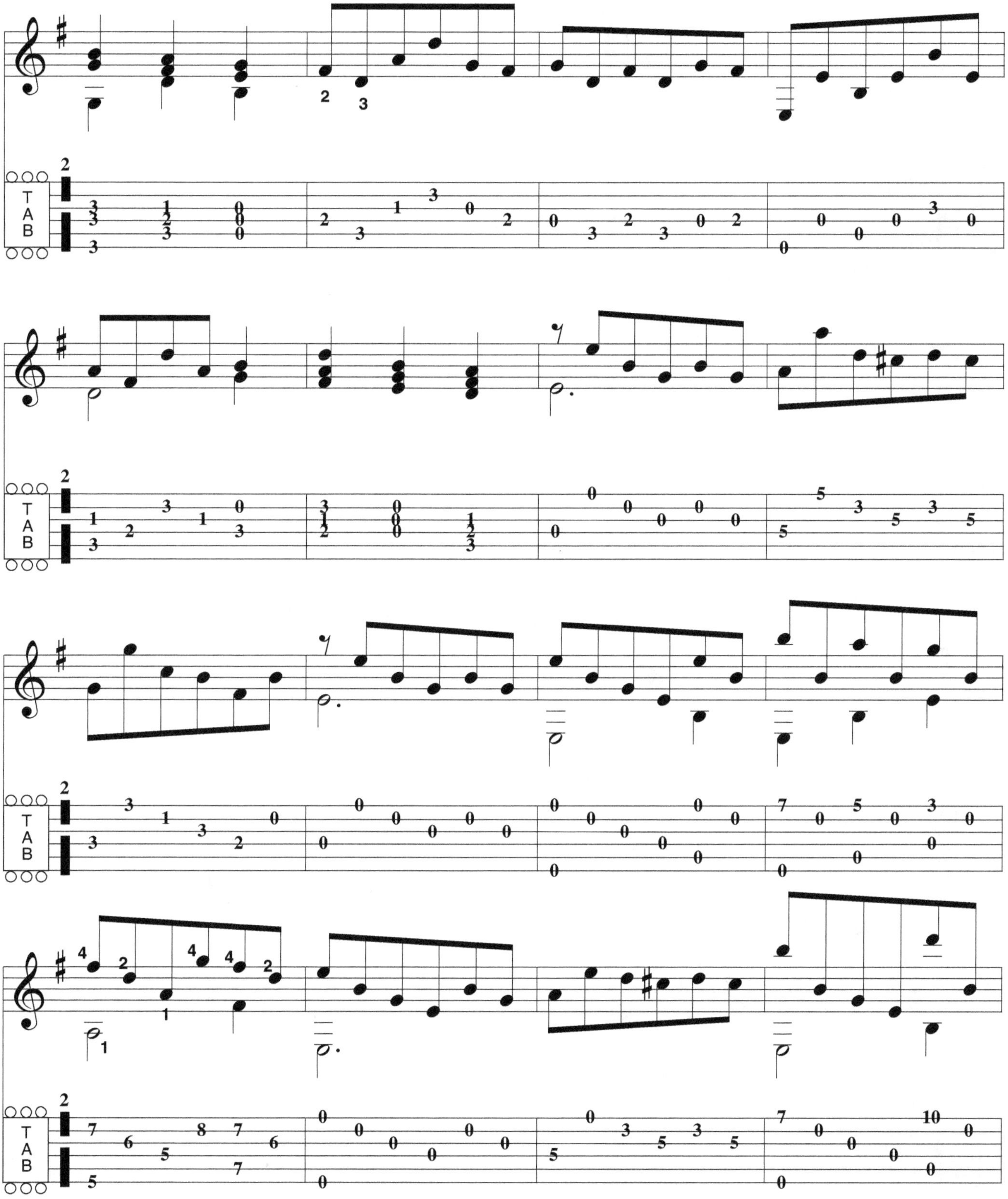
T
A
B

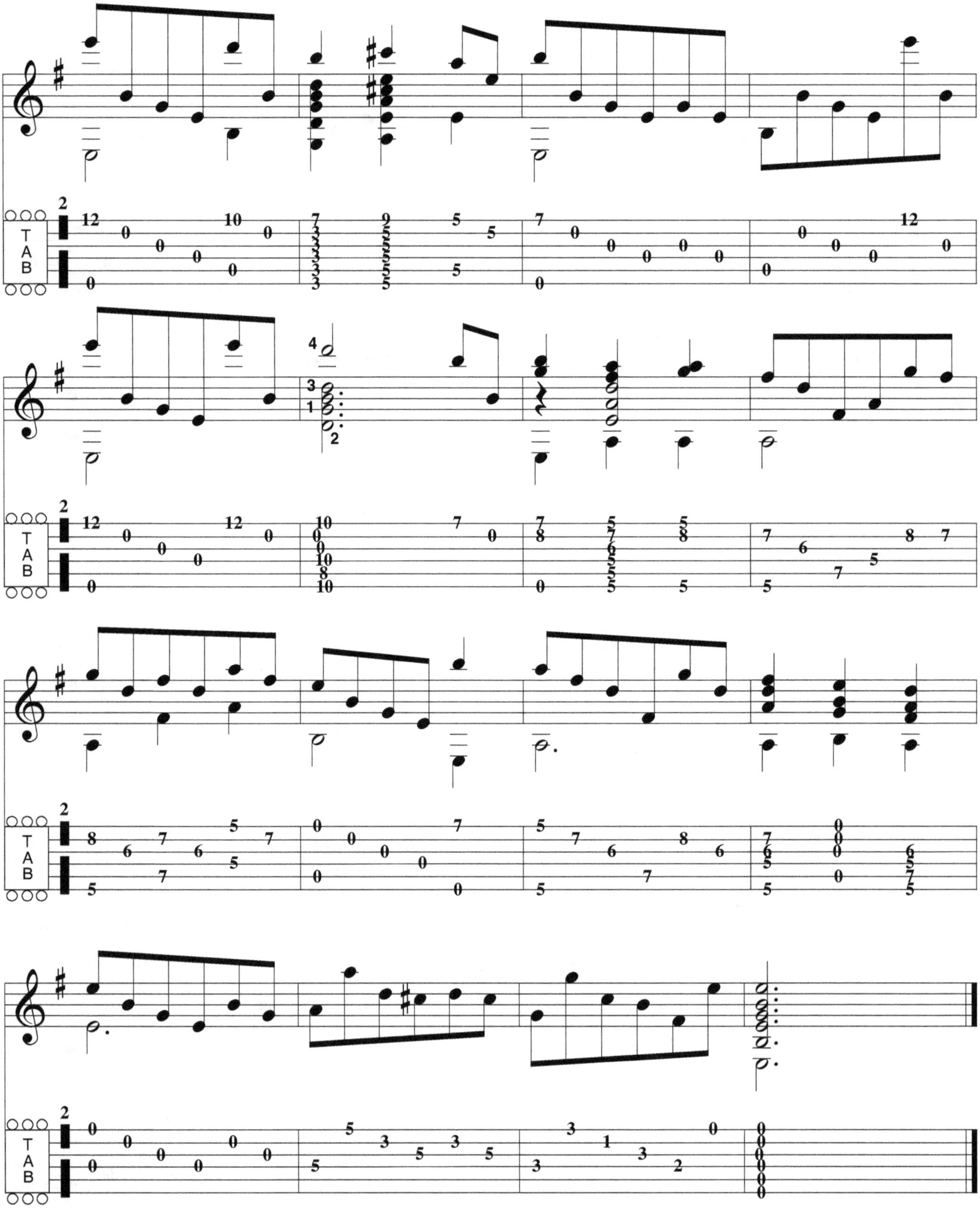

GREENSLEEVES

Trad.

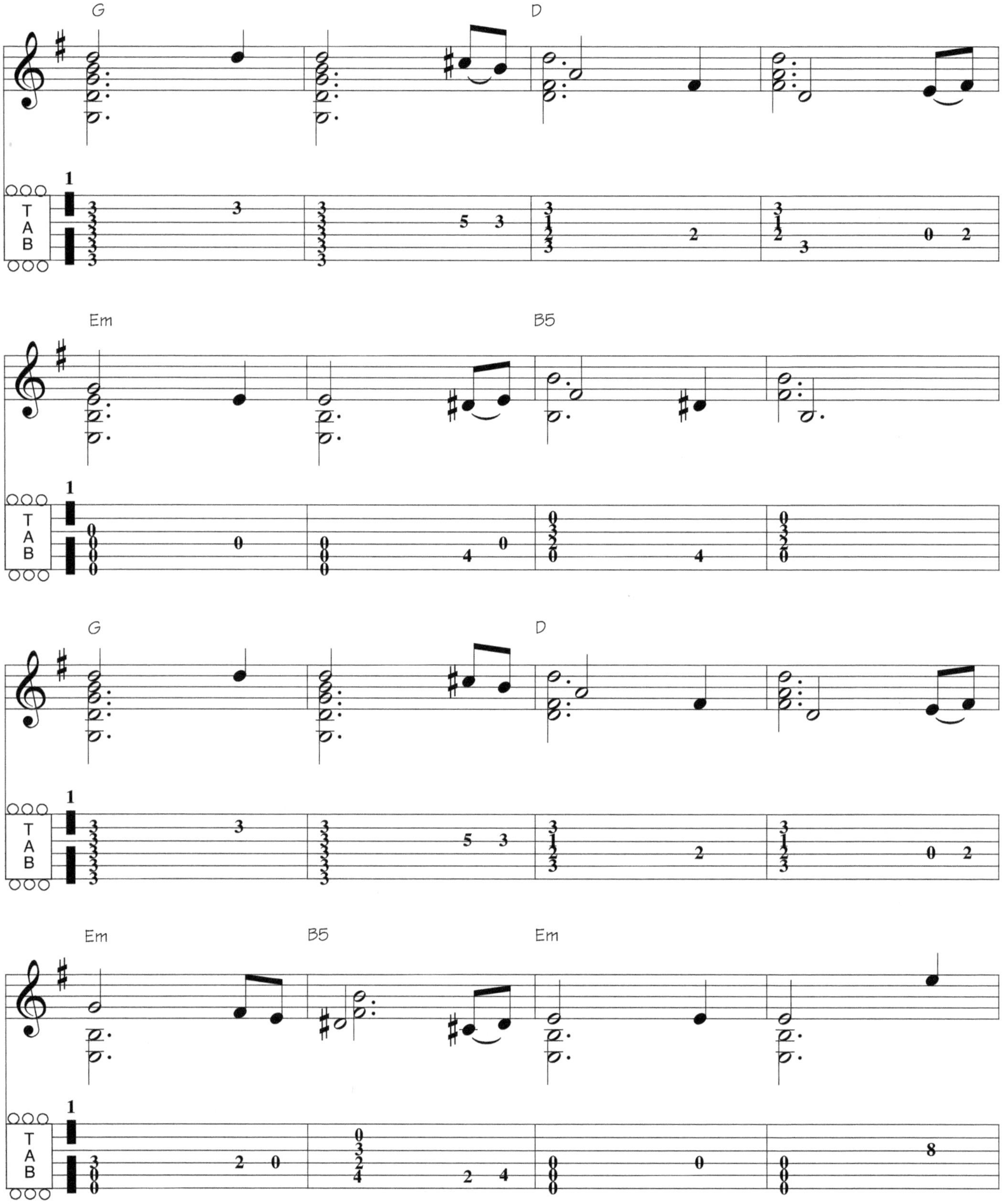
G
D
Em
B5
G
D
Em
B5
Em
TAB

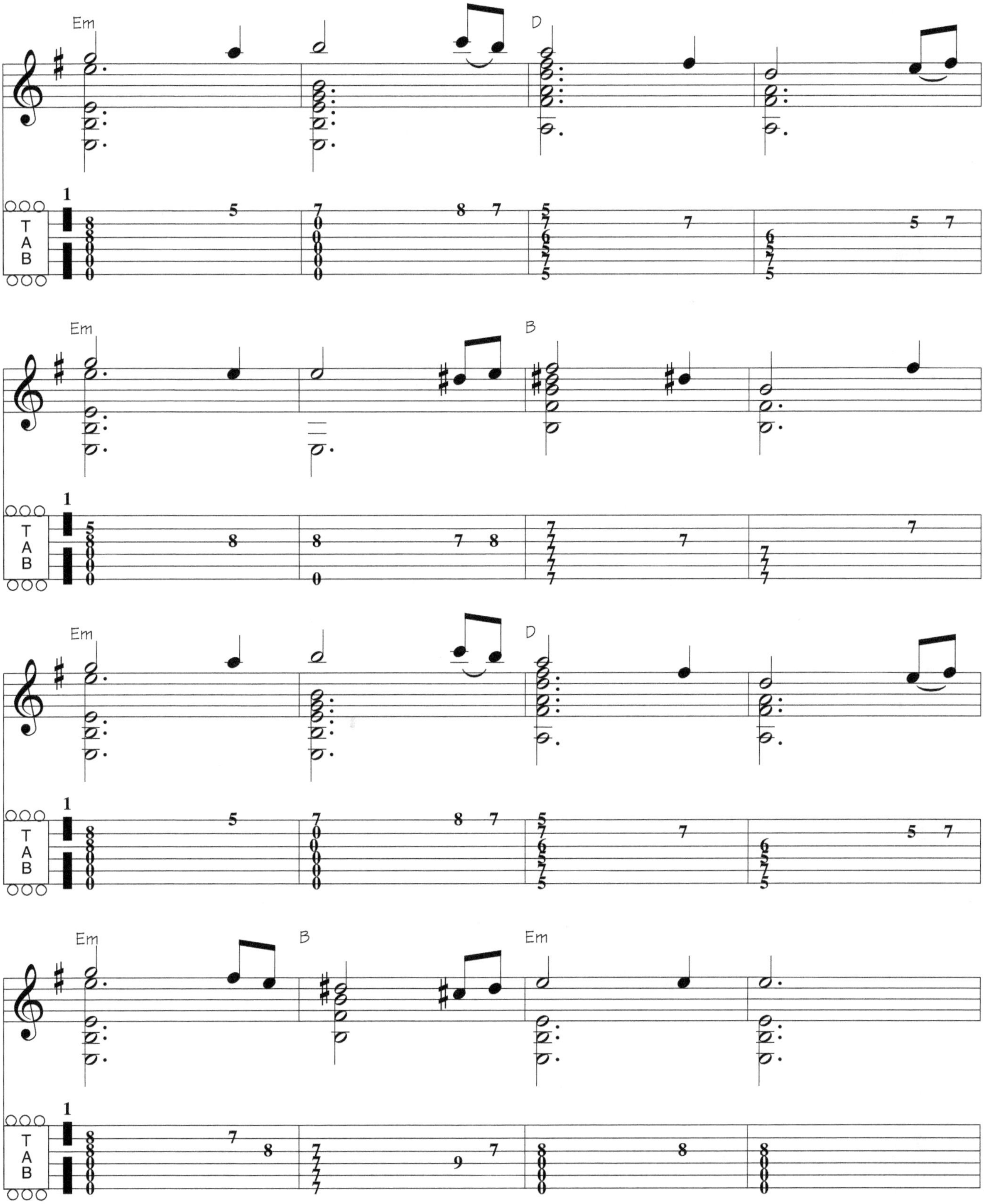
Em
D
Em
B
Em
D
Em
B
Em
TAB

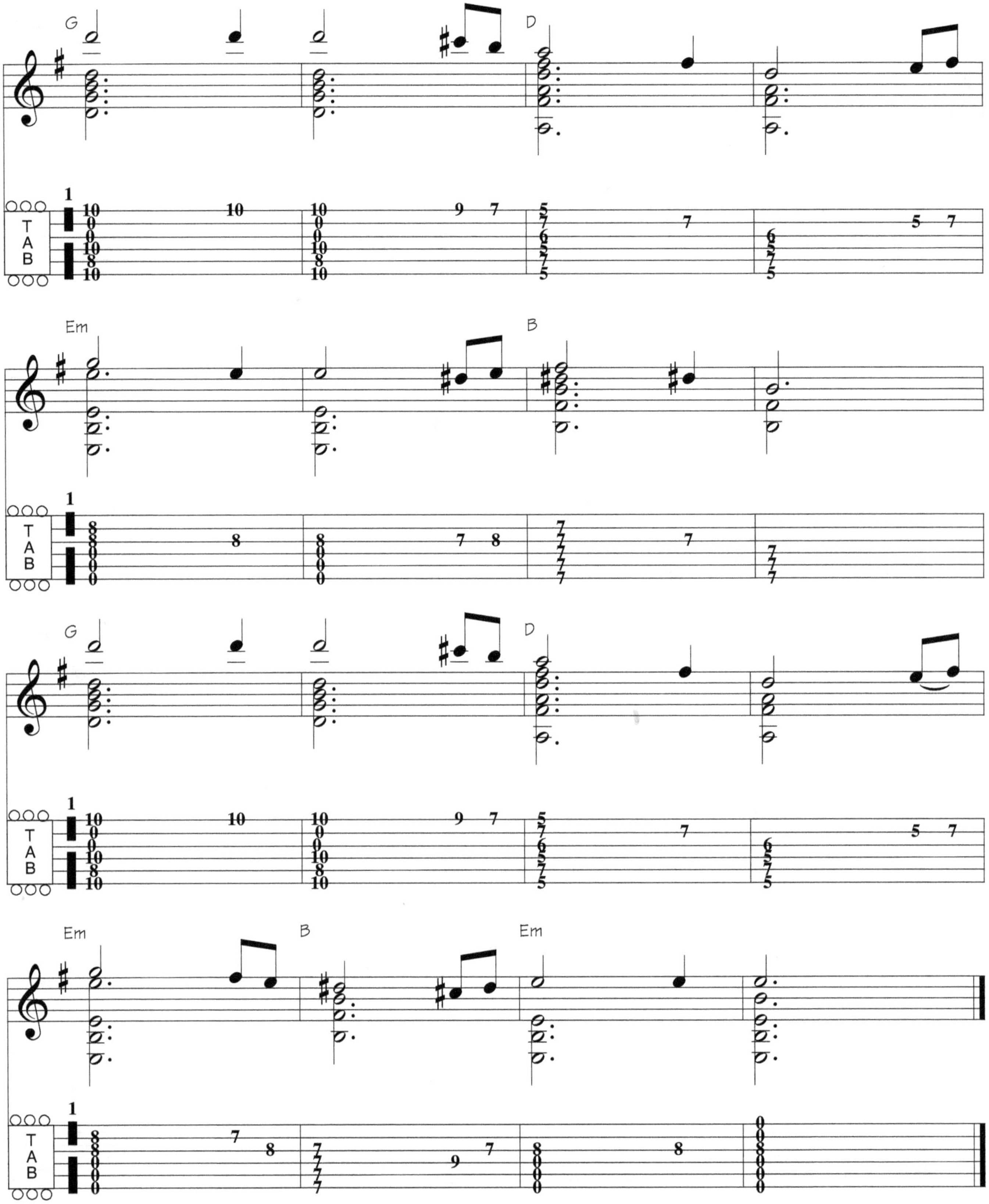
G
D
Em
B
G
D
Em
B
Em
TAB

SAILOR'S HORNPIPE

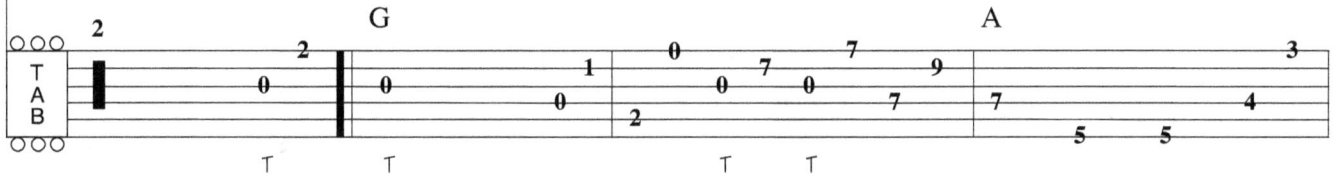

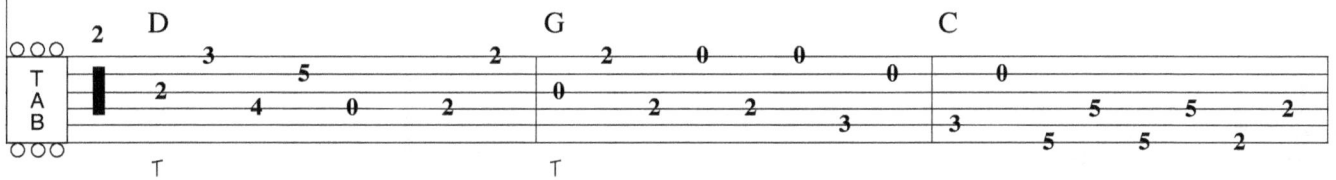

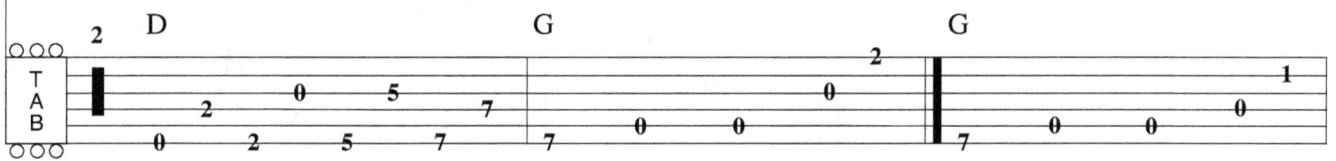

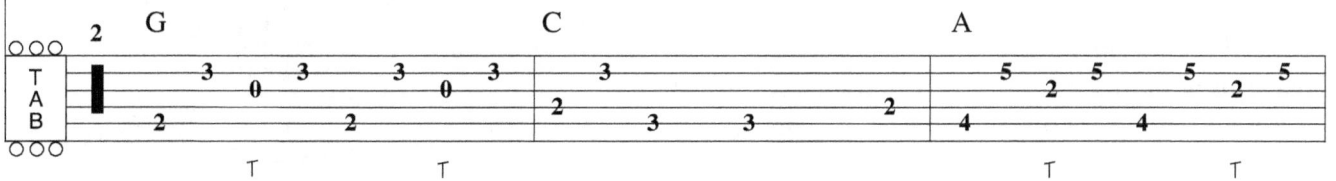

Sailor's Hornpipe

The mechanics of this arrangement are much like the way "melodic" banjo style works, though on the 12-string, the octave strings act like the 5th string of the banjo. The tunes can be played very fast, and the lingering resonances of the notes create an effect reminiscent of a hammered dulcimer. In measures 6 and 7, and also in 15 and 16, the right-hand fingers must play the notes on the D or 4th string. Otherwise, all notes on the top three strings are played by the fingers, and all bass notes by the thumb. Depending on which side of the pair of strings you strike, you can get either of the pair to dominate. A light touch will allow just one half of the pair to ring, and a stronger attack will sound both of them. On 12-string, it is probably best to play this with fingerpicks or very good nails, since it is hard to get bare fingers between the pairs of strings.

WARNING!!! This only works on a 12-string or Nashville-strung guitar...

FISHER'S HORNPIPE

Trad.

Fisher's Hornpipe

This works in the same manner as "*Sailor's Hornpipe*", and features the unusual, chromatic-style picking. The left hand has to work pretty hard on this one, although you can simplify things a little and people won't complain. There is nothing in the whole world of guitar that sounds anything like this, and if you normally play a 12-string, and are a pretty good fingerpicker, you'll have people running from across the room to see what you are doing once you get this one down. You'll probably have your 12-string tuned down a couple frets, so this will sound in G if you do or A otherwise. Fiddlers play it in D.

WARNING!!! This only works on a 12-string or Nashville-strung guitar...

FÜR ELISE

L. V. Beethoven

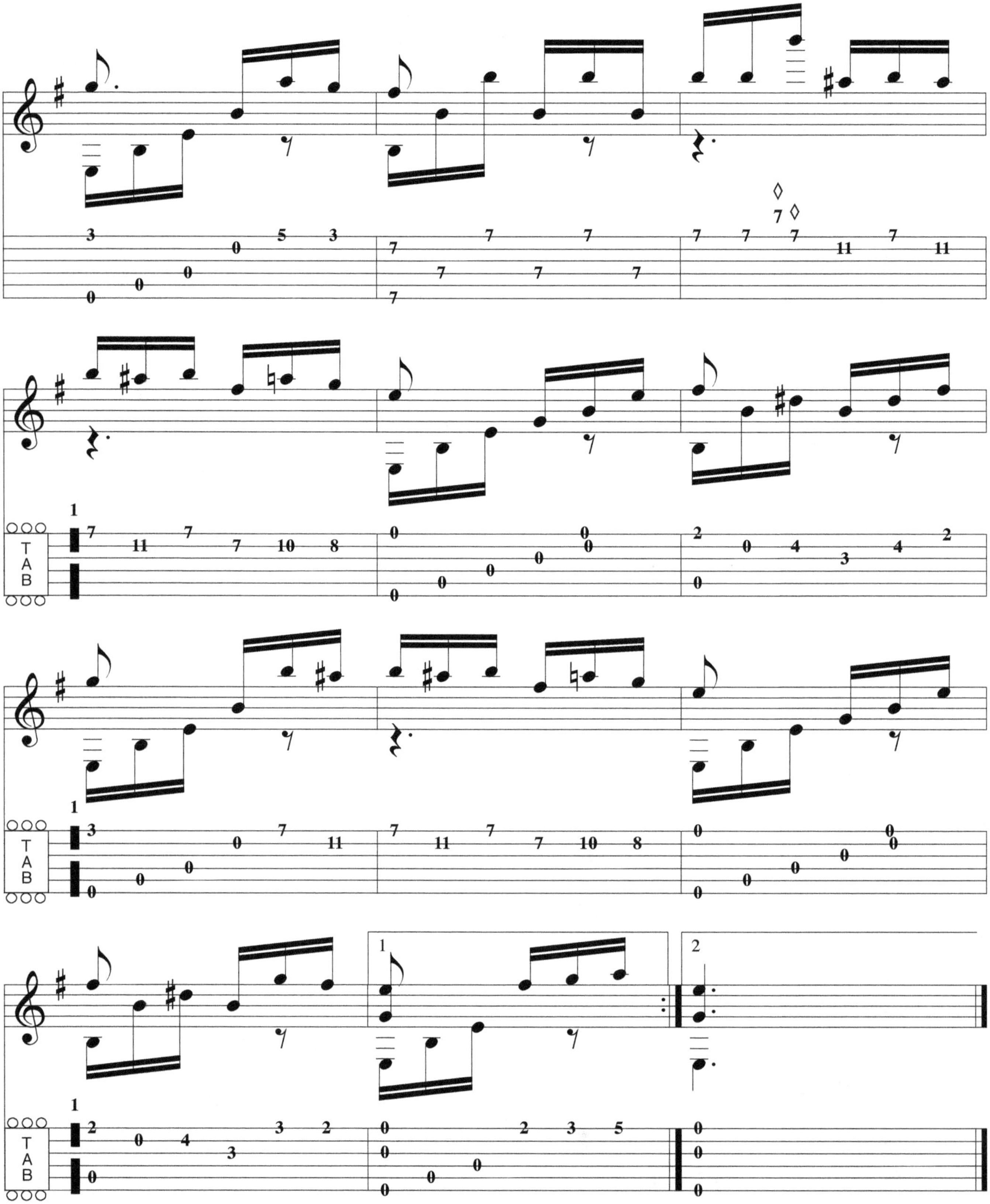
TAB

Für Elise

This transcription of the familiar Beethoven piano piece was taken note-for-note from a keyboard arrangement, without any alteration. It's not at all difficult, and the large number of open strings, such as in measure 3, give the arrangement a very natural and flowing sound. The stretch in measure 12 is the hardest part, and the harmonic (◊) in measure 15 can be played at the 7th fret or as a right-hand harmonic at the 19th fret. (Touch the harmonic with the index finger of the right hand and pluck it with the thumb.) This allows the V chord barred at the 7th fret to sustain.)

Be sure your guitar is tuned to the E-minus configuration. (See page 34.) There is probably no other way to play this lovely tune on guitar without changing or omitting notes, or using very awkward fingerings.

Suite in F: For the Duchess

This is a three-part suite, probably the first guitar piece ever written in the *E-suspended* partial capo configuration. It makes good use of the open-string possibilities offered by the partial capo, and allows melodies and bass lines to be played together against sustaining open strings. Parts I and II are structurally the same as traditional fiddle tunes, with AABB format. They both allow distinctive melodic runs in a "harp-like" manner, with successive notes on different strings. Part II is slower and very baroque.

On my first recording of this in 1984, the guitar had capo 1, which put the pitch in F and made the sound a little sweeter. (Hence the name of the piece.) I usually perform it in E, but my guitar is often tuned a fret low so it sometimes sounds in Eb. The best-known recording of it from *Solo Guitar Sketchbook* CD in 1989 is played in E. That version was remastered in 2010 and re-released on the *Capo Voodoo: Solo Guitar* CD.

SUITE IN F: FOR THE DUCHESS- PART 1

H. Reid

PART 2

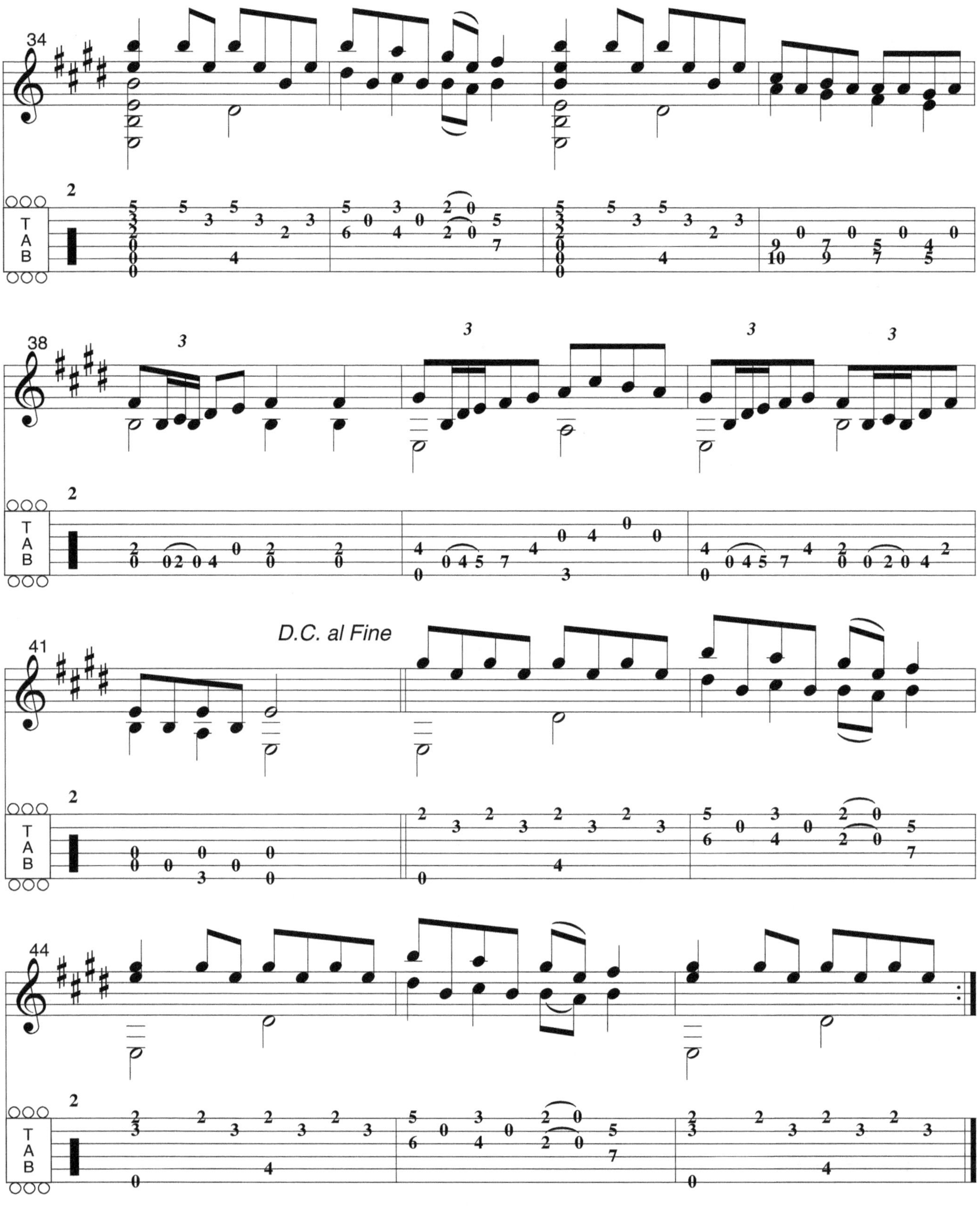
D.C. al Fine

PART 3

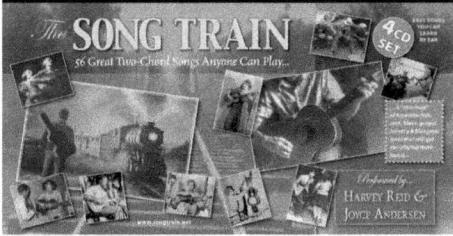

THE SONG TRAIN (2007) is a landmark resource for beginning guitarists by Harvey Reid & Joyce Andersen. 4-CD boxed set with 80-page color hardback book, contains 56 one & two chord songs. Half the songs are copyrighted, by the likes of Bob Dylan, Hank Williams, Chuck Berry etc, so it offers beginners easy but great songs they can play. Folk, blues, gospel, rock, celtic, country and gospel songs, and an amazing cross-section of American music. **www.songtrain.net**

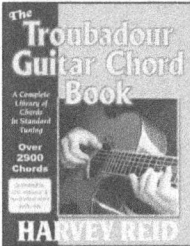

THE TROUBADOUR GUITAR CHORD BOOK (2013) The best, most complete and readable standard-tuning chord encyclopedia, and an essential new reference tool. A monumental and important new work that may never go back on your shelf. Unlike other large chord books that are tailored for jazz guitarists, the *Troubadour Guitar Chord Book* features over 2900 open and closed-string voicings, optimized and selected for solo acoustic and troubadour-style guitarists.

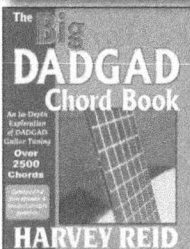

THE BIG DADGAD CHORD BOOK (2014) The best, most complete and readable chord encyclopedia in DADGAD tuning, with 2500 chords mapped out. Another indispensable reference book for anyone who plays in this popular tuning. Also features full-fingerboard diagrams, with every note and scale degree shown for every chord.

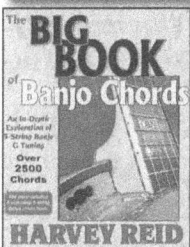

THE BIG BOOK OF BANJO CHORDS (2015) The most complete, detailed and versatile book of chords for standard banjo G tuning. The fingerboard shown like never before, with 5th string notes shown.

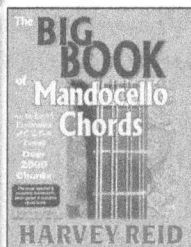

THE BIG BOOK OF MANDOCELLO CHORDS (2015) The most complete, detailed and versatile book of chords for standard C-G-A-D tuning. Also includes 11 of the first ideas ever published for partial capos on mandocello.

THE BIG BOOK OF BARITONE UKULELE CHORDS (2015) The most complete, detailed and versatile book of chords for standard D-G-B-E tuning.

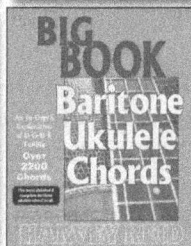

BARITONE UKULELE SIMPLIFIED (2015) Explores 9 different new tunings and partial capo ideas that reveal for the first time how to play instant music with great-sounding but simpler chord shapes.

SLEIGHT OF HAND (1983) The first book of partial capo guitar arrangements, still in print. 16 solo guitar arrangements using a universal partial capo. Intermediate to advanced level, mostly for fingerstyle guitar, but has 2 flatpicked fiddle tune arrangements (*Sally Goodin'* and *Devil's Dream*) In TAB and standard notation. *Suite: For the Duchess, Für Elise, Scarborough Fair, Minuet in Dm, Flowers of Edinburgh, Simple Gifts, Sally Goodin', Irish Washerwoman, Pavanne, Minuet in Dm, Red-Haired Boy, June Apple, Jesu Joy of Man's Desiring, Devil's Dream, Sally Goodin', Scherzo, Shenandoah, Greensleeves, Sailor's Hornpipe, Fisher's Hornpipe*

CAPO INVENTIONS (2006) 14 intermediate to advanced arrangements from Reid's catalog of guitar recordings. Precisely transcribed for solo guitar, these pieces all use a 3-string *Esus* type partial capo. In TAB and standard notation. *Skye Boat Song, Highwire Hornpipe, Windy Grave, Hard Times, The Unknown Soldier, Suite: For the Duchess, The Arkansas Traveler, The Minstrel Boy, Red in the Sky, Prelude to the Minstrel's Dream, Norway Suite: Parts 1 &2, Star Island Jig, Macallan's Jig.*

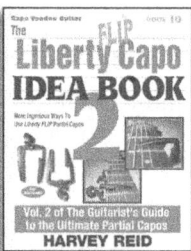

THE LIBERTY "FLIP" CAPO IDEA BOOKS (2014-15) Two volumes, totaling almost 400 pages, with over 113 ideas of partial capo configurations that can be done with a pair of *Model 43* and *Model 65 Liberty* partial capos. These were developed by Harvey Reid, and are the new generation of sleek and versatile partial capos that clamp 6, 5, 4 or 3 strings on most guitars, banjos, ukes and mandolins. Volume I shows 72 ideas, mostly in standard tuning, and with a taste of combining capos with altered tunings. Volume 2 combines capos with altered tunings.

SECRETS OF THE 3-STRING PARTIAL CAPO (2010) 24 mind-bending ways to use the popular 3-string *Esus* (*E-suspended*) type partial capo. *This book may no longer be available after the arrival of the Liberty Capos.* **18 of these ideas are now in the *Liberty Capo IDEA BOOK* , and the other 6 appear in the *Liberty "FLIP" Capo IDEA BOOK Vol.2*.**

MORE SECRETS OF THE 3-STRING PARTIAL CAPO (2013) 27 more ways to use 3-string *Esus* (*E-suspended*) type partial capos. **12 of these ideas are now in the *Liberty Capo IDEA BOOK* , and the others are in the *Liberty Capo IDEA BOOK Vol.2*.**

SECRETS OF THE 4 & 5-STRING PARTIAL CAPOS (2011) Another treasure trove of ideas, for the *Planet Waves, Shubb,* or *Kyser* shortened 4 or 5-string capos. (Also valuable for *Third Hand, Liberty "Flip"* or *Spider* universal capos.) Most people who have one of these capos know a few ways to use them. Here are an amazing 47 ideas that use a 4 or 5-string capo to generate new music. Over 1600 chords. *This book may no longer be available after the arrival of the Liberty Capos.* **30 of these 47 ideas are now in the *Liberty Capo IDEA BOOK* , and the other 17 appear in the *Liberty Capo IDEA BOOK Vol.2*.**

SECRETS OF THE 1 & 2-STRING PARTIAL CAPOS (2012) How to use the unique *Woodie's G-Band* 1 and 2-string partial capos. 33 clever ways to use these capos in a number of tunings and in combination with other partial capos, with over 1100 chords. 98 pages are packed with photos, ideas and capo knowledge that is only available here. Even the makers of the capos don't know about these ideas.

SECRETS OF PARTIAL CAPOS IN DADGAD TUNING (2012) Most people think of partial capos as a substitute for open tunings, and don't realize that they can be combined. Harvey Reid shows you over 25 ingenious ways to use partial capos to expand the musical possibilities of DADGAD tuning (4 of them use the similar CGDGAD tuning.) Get new chords, fingerings, voicings, resonances and unlock a new, mysterious world of new music hiding in your fingerboard. **17 of these ideas are now in the *Liberty Capo IDEA BOOK Vol.2*.**

SECRETS OF UNIVERSAL PARTIAL CAPOS (2012) 45 ways to get new music from your guitar that can only be done with universal partial capos. This hidden world of music in your fingerboard includes a number of tunings and combinations with other partial capos. Over 1500 chords. Packed with photos, clear explanations and capo strategy will save you years of searching. **Because the *Model 43 Liberty* capo clamps 4 middle strings, 13 of these ideas are now duplicated in the *Liberty Capo IDEA BOOKS, Vol. 1-2*.**

SECRETS OF PARTIAL CAPOS IN DROP D TUNING (2014) The most common tuning is *Drop D*: D A D G B E, and like any tuning, it can be combined with partial capos to add another dimension to the guitar. This book presents 24 ways to use one or more partial capos of all types to generate more new music. **9 of these ideas are now in the *Liberty Capo IDEA BOOK*, and 7 more appear in *Vol.2*.** The others use a universal or *G-Band* capo.

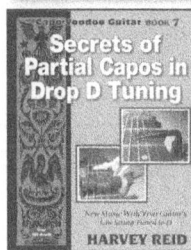

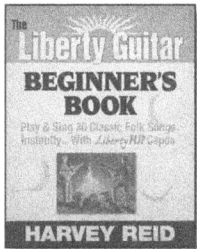

THE LIBERTY GUITAR BEGINNER'S BOOK (2015) Play 30 classic folk songs instantly with super-simple, great-sounding chords. For children or adults, this book carefully explains how to use *Liberty Tuning* to play chords and sing songs in 6 different major and minor keys. You need a guitar, a full capo, and a *Liberty FLIP Model 43* capo.

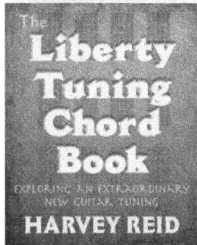

THE LIBERTY TUNING CHORD BOOK (2013) In his partial capo research, Harvey Reid discovered a simple new guitar tuning that introduces a remarkable geometrical symmetry and simplicity to the guitar fingerboard that no one ever dreamed existed. Here is a thorough examination of what this amazing tuning can do, with over 1200 chords, sorted, mapped out and organized to help you find your way in *Liberty Tuning*. Lots of tips, advice & clear explanations. For guitar teachers, beginners and anyone who already plays guitar and wants to learn about this important discovery.

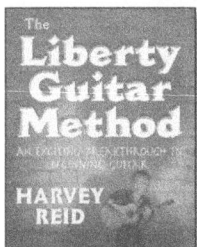

THE LIBERTY GUITAR METHOD (2013) Total beginners can play music like never before. It's easy to do and sounds great. Learn to use *Liberty Tuning* to play great-sounding, simple 2-finger chords to songs by Bob Dylan, Hank Williams, John Prine, Johnny Cash, Chuck Berry, The Beatles, Adele, and more. You won't believe it 'til you try it. *Hush Little Baby, This Land is Your Land, Your Cheating Heart, A Hard Rain's A Gonna Fall, Amazing Grace, The Cuckoo, Folsom Prison Blues, Angel From Montgomery, Maybellene, Let It Be, Imagine, Someone Like You, The Wedding Song, House of the Rising Sun*

THE LIBERTY SONG TRAIN (2013) Learn how to use *Liberty Tuning* to play all 56 two-chord songs in the epic *Song Train* collection with just 2-finger chords, in the same keys as they were done on the *Song Train* recordings. Beginning guitar has never been easier. Careful explanations, with lots of helpful tips, strategy and advice. If you have the *Song Train* 4-CD collection, you need this companion book.

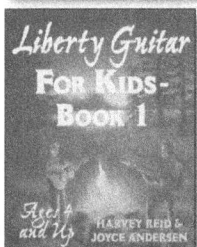

LIBERTY GUITAR FOR KIDS (2013) It's a huge breakthrough in children's guitar. Children as young as 4 can learn to strum simple 2-finger *Liberty Tuning* chords and play guitar like never before. Classic traditional plus modern children's songs arranged in keys young voices can sing in. No need to wait until the children grow bigger or waste your money on crummy small children's guitars. Learn how even small children can instantly start strumming songs on adult guitars. It's really amazing. *London Bridge, Row Row Row Your Boat, Farmer in the Dell, Hush Little Baby, This Land is Your Land, Oh Susannah, Standing in the Need of Prayer, Hey Lolly Lolly, Comin' Round the Mountain* and more.

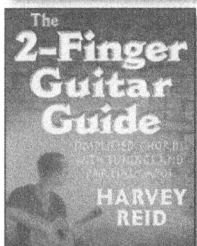

THE 2-FINGER GUITAR GUIDE (2013) A careful study of simplified guitar chords, this book takes you through each of the common tunings and partial capo configurations that can be used to play simplified guitar chords. Learn the advantages and disadvantages of each of 28 different guitar environments, including the amazing *Liberty Tuning* and related hybrid tunings. If you have a shortage of fingers on the fretting hand, or if you work with hand injuries, special music education or music therapy, this is the definitive guide to showing what can be done musically with just 2 finger chords.

ABOUT THE AUTHOR

Harvey Reid has been a full-time acoustic guitar player since 1974, and has performed over 6000 concerts throughout the US and in Europe. He won the 1981 *National Fingerpicking Guitar Competition* and the 1982 *International Autoharp* contest, and has released 32 highly-acclaimed recordings of original, traditional and contemporary acoustic music.

He is best known for his solo fingerstyle guitar work, but he is also a solid flatpicker (he won Bill Monroe's *Beanblossom* bluegrass guitar contest in 1976), a versatile singer, lyricist, prolific composer, arranger and songwriter. He also plays mandolin and bouzouki. Reid recorded the first album ever of 6 & 12-string banjo music, and his CD **Solo Guitar Sketchbook** made GUITAR PLAYER MAGAZINE's Top 20 essential acoustic guitar CD's list. His CD **Steel Drivin' Man** was chosen by ACOUSTIC GUITAR MAGAZINE as one of **Top 10 Folk CD's** of all time, along with Woody Guthrie, Ry Cooder and other hallowed names. His music was included in the blockbuster BBC TV show *A Musical Tour of Scotland*, and Reid was featured in the Rhino Records **Acoustic Music of the 90's** collection, along with a "who's who" line-up of other artists including Richard Thompson, Jerry Garcia & Leo Kottke.

In 1980 Reid published *A New Frontier in Guitar,* the first book about the partial capo, and in 1984 he wrote **Modern Folk Guitar**, the first college textbook for folk guitar. Quite possibly the first modern person to publish and record with the partial capo, he is almost certainly the most prolific arranger and composer of partial capo guitar music, and is responsible for most of what is known about the device. He lives in southern Maine with his family.

Harvey Reid in 1982